FIT'S FOR SUPPER?

Compiled by The Reading Bus

with illustrations by Bob Dewar

Published in the United Kingdom in 2009 by

Reading Bus Press

Reading Bus Depot, Kittybrewster School, Great Northern Road, Aberdeen AB24 3QG

ISBN 978-0-9558904-9-9

www.readingbus.co.uk

Project managed by Jenny Watson, Reading Bus Co-ordinator with
assistance from Jayne Addison, Reading Bus Administrator and Sheila Lawtie, Health Co-ordinator

Technical advice and support from Donna Knight, Product Assessment Executive, Tesco Stores Limited

Recipes contributed from a variety of sources including Royal Highland Show, entries from Tesco Stores Limited
Recipe Competition, St Peter's RC School, Dewar, Gordon and Watson kitchens

Designed by Julie Barclay

Printed by Scotprint, Haddington

A catalogue record for this book is available from the British Library

CONTENTS

TOMATO AND RED PEPPER SOUP

Serves 4

Preparation Time: 5 minutes

Cooking Time: 20 minutes

YOU WILL NEED

2 x 15ml spoons (2 tablespoons) olive oil

1 onion, peeled and chopped

2 red peppers, deseeded and chopped

8 large ripe tomatoes, chopped

600ml (1 pint) chicken stock

5 basil leaves, shredded

1. Put the butter in a deep pan and heat, add the onion and cook for five minutes till it is soft. Add the garlic and the potato and mix everything together.

2. Now add the lettuce and the stock and a little black pepper. Simmer for twenty minutes. Remove from the heat, allow to cool a little then blend with a hand blender.

3. When this is done add the cream, or the crème fraiche. This will melt as soon as it hits the soup. Stir through. Check seasoning - in other words, have a little taste. You might want to add a little salt or more black pepper.

4. Reheat the soup and after you've served it into bowls, garnish each one with a sprinkling of chopped mint.

This recipe also works well with watercress. Just use one pack of watercress instead of lettuce. It tastes a little more peppery.

CREAM OF LETTUCE SOUP

Serves 4
Preparation Time: 10 minutes
Cooking Time: 25 minutes

SIX

SOUPS

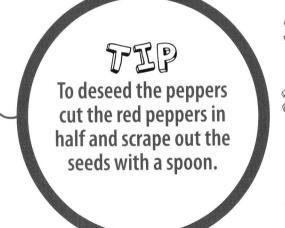
1. Put the oil in a deep pan and heat, add the onion and cook for about five minutes till it is soft.

2. Add the peppers and the tomatoes, cook for another five minutes, stirring so that everything is mixed.

3. Add the stock and simmer gently for ten minutes.

4. You can leave this soup chunky and serve it like that or, you can blend it with a hand blender. If you're going to do that, take it off the heat and allow it to cool a little first. Then reheat it.

5. Just before serving tear up some basil leaves into smallish pieces and drop them in. Basil always tastes better if you tear it up rather than chop it.

CARROT AND LENTIL SOUP

Serves 4
Preparation Time: 5 minutes
Cooking Time: 25 minutes

1. Put the oil into a deep pan, heat and add the onions. Cook for five minutes till they are soft then pop in the carrots and stir so they are coated with the oil.

2. Sprinkle in the coriander and lentils and give everything a good stir. It should be smelling quite good by now.

3. Now, pour in the stock and bring to the boil. Then turn down the heat and simmer gently for about twenty minutes.

4. You can serve this soup just as it is or you can blend it with a hand blender. Remember to let it cool a little before you do this. Reheat and serve.

YOU WILL NEED

2 x 15ml spoons (2 tablespoons) olive oil

1 onion, peeled and chopped

6 large carrots, washed, peeled and sliced

1 x 5ml spoon (1 teaspoon) of ground coriander

200g (8oz) split red lentils

900ml (1½ pint) vegetable stock

GREEN PEA AND MINT SOUP

Serves 4
Preparation Time: 2 minutes
Cooking Time: 10 minutes

MINT

1. Put the stock into a pan, bring to the boil, pour in the peas, add the mint and simmer for ten minutes.

2. Take off the heat, cool then blend with a hand blender, and serve. That's it.

How easy is that. You can add a dollop of crème fraiche if you like, and you can add a clove of garlic. You don't have to crush it as you're going to blend everything at the end.

SWEET POTATO AND BUTTERNUT SQUASH SOUP

Serves 4
Preparation Time: 10 minutes
Cooking Time: 30 minutes

YOU WILL NEED

2 x 15ml spoons (2 tablespoons) olive oil

2 onions, peeled and chopped

1 butternut squash, peeled and chopped into cubes

2 sweet potatoes, peeled and chopped into cubes

600ml (1 pint) chicken stock

50ml (2 fl oz) crème fraiche

2 x 5ml spoons (2 teaspoons) fresh chopped parsley

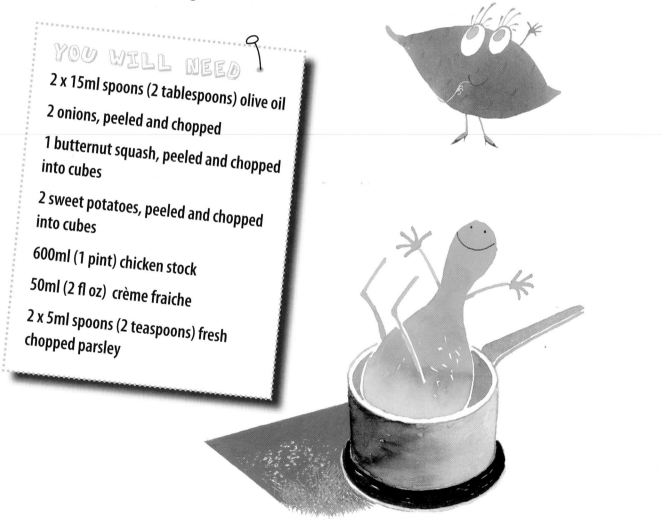

1. Put the oil into a deep pan, heat a little, add the onions and cook for about five minutes till they are soft.

2. Add the squash and sweet potato and cook over a low heat for about ten minutes. Give them a stir now and then.

3. Add the stock and simmer gently for twenty minutes till everything is soft.

4. Remove from the heat, allow to cool a little then blend with a hand blender.

5. Put the soup back on the cooker and heat through. Serve it with a dollop of crème fraiche and a scattering of chopped parsley on top of each bowl.

SCOTCH BROTH

Serves 6
Preparation Time: 15 minutes
Cooking Time: 1 hour 10 minutes

YOU WILL NEED

2x 15ml spoons (2 tablespoons) olive oil

2 onions, peeled and chopped

1 clove garlic, chopped

200g (7oz) lamb leg steak, chopped finely

2 carrots, washed and diced

1 small turnip, peeled and cut into cubes

2 celery sticks, washed and chopped finely

1 large potato, peeled and diced

1 leek, washed and chopped finely

black pepper to taste

50g (2oz) pearl barley

1.5 litres (2 pints) lamb stock

2 x 5ml spoons (2 teapoons) fresh parsley, chopped

1. Put the oil into a pan, add the chopped onions and cook for about five minutes till the onions are soft. Add the crushed garlic and lamb. Cook until the lamb is brown all over.

2. Add all the other vegetables and move them about the pan with a wooden spoon till they are all coated in the oil. Cook for about ten minutes till they are soft.

3. It's time to season everything. Add a little pepper. Your stock, if you are using a cube, will have salt in it. Best to wait till the end before adding more. See what it tastes like, first.

4. Wash the pearl barley and add it to the pan.

5. Add the stock and let the soup simmer for fifty minutes.

6. Before serving add chopped parsley.

PUMPKIN SOUP

Serves 6
Preparation Time: 10 minutes
Cooking Time: 35 minutes

YOU WILL NEED

1 pumpkin, roughly 450g (1lb)

1 x 15ml spoon (1 tablespoon) olive oil

1 onion, chopped

1 clove garlic, chopped

300ml (1/2 pint) milk

600ml (1 pint) vegetable stock

black pepper to taste

2 x 5ml spoons (2 teaspoons) fresh parsley, chopped

Pumpkins are so lovely, it seems a shame to cut them open and eat them. But there you go, if you want the soup, it has to be done. This soup has a velvety texture.

1. First get the flesh out of the pumpkin. The best way to do this is to cut it in half, then quarters. Now take away the seeds and when that's done, cut out the flesh and cut it into cubes. Or just bits.

2. Put the olive oil into a pan and heat a little. Add the chopped onion and cook slowly for about four to five minutes before adding the garlic and the pumpkin.

3. Let them all cook for another five minutes so that they can get friendly. And, so that their flavours can seep into the pan and mingle.

4. Now add the milk, and after that the stock. Let all this slowly simmer for twenty five minutes.

5. Take it off the heat and let it cool, then blend with a hand blender. Season with black pepper. Reheat before serving into bowls with a good scattering of parsley on top.

If you like spicy food, you can add a teaspoon of curry mix when the vegetables are simmering and instead of milk you can use a can of coconut milk.

TIP

Chopping an onion isn't as hard as it looks. First cut off the top and bottom and peel the skin. Cut it in half and put the flat side down on your chopping board. Cut it in slices from top to bottom. Then trying to keep it all together, turn it round and cut it in more slices across the way. When you let go, you'll have lots of little bits of onion. Don't worry if at the end you have some big onion chunks, you can cut them up, too.

MAINS

MEATBALLS IN TOMATO SAUCE

Serves 4
Preparation Time: 10 minutes
Cooking Time: 15 minutes

Heat the oven to 180C, 350F or GAS 4

1. Put the pork, the beef, the onion, garlic, the breadcrumbs and the egg into a bowl and season with a little salt and a grating of black pepper. Mix up with your hands, squishing everything together till it's a big gooey mass.

2. Taking a bit out at a time, roll into walnut sized balls. This is like playing with plasticine, rolling the mix between your palms. As each meatball is made, put it onto a lightly greased baking tray. When they're all finished put the tray into the oven and cook for fifteen minutes.

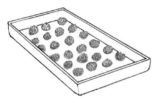

3. Meanwhile put the passata into a saucepan and simmer for ten minutes. Tear the basil into shreds and drop it into the sauce and cook for a further five minutes.

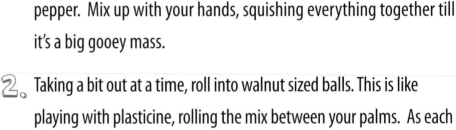

4. When the meatballs are ready, take them out of the oven and gently put them into the sauce.

Serve with spaghetti or any pasta shape, cooked to the back of the pack instructions.

YOU WILL NEED

150g (5oz) minced pork

150g (5oz) minced beef

1 onion, peeled and chopped

2 garlic cloves, crushed

25g (1oz) breadcrumbs

1 egg lightly beaten,

pinch of salt and pepper to taste

1 jar of passata (or can of chopped tomatoes)

2 x 5ml spoons (2 teaspoons) fresh basil, shredded

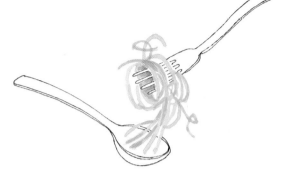

HAWAIIAN HADDOCK

Heat the oven to 180C, 350F, GAS 4

1. Put the potatoes in a pan of slightly salted water. Bring to the boil and simmer for twelve to eighteen minutes. After twelve minutes test them with a fork, if the fork slides in easily they are ready, if not boil for another two minutes and try again.

2. While they are boiling prepare your fish. Put the fish in a pan and cover with the milk. Gently bring to the boil and simmer for about eight minutes till the fish is cooked. Take off the heat and allow to cool a little.

3. Carefully lift the fish out of the milk and put in a bowl. Remove the oily skin from the fish. Keep two tablespoons of the milk. Flake up the fish with a fork and add the crème fraiche. Stir together.

4. Put the pineapple into an ovenproof dish and spread your creamy fishy mixture on top.

5. Drain your potatoes and mash them with a potato masher. Then add the two tablespoons of the milk that the fish was cooked in and beat well with a wooden spoon. Season this with grated pepper and a pinch of nutmeg.

6. Put the mashed potatoes on top of the fishy spread. Sprinkle the grated cheese over the potato topping. Into the oven it goes for twenty minutes till it has turned golden.

Serves 4
Preparation Time: 20 minutes
Cooking Time: 20 minutes

YOU WILL NEED

3 or 4 potatoes peeled

4 smoked haddock

100ml (4fl oz) semi skimmed milk

150ml (5fl oz) crème fraiche

1 x 225g (8oz) can crushed pineapple

black pepper to taste

1 pinch of nutmeg

50g (2oz) grated cheddar cheese

PLOUGHBOY'S FEAST

This is a hearty dish. To make it, you cook three things separately - leeks, mince and potatoes. Then you put them together in layers in an ovenproof dish before putting it in the oven for thirty minutes.

Serves 4
Preparation Time: 30 minutes
Cooking Time: 30 minutes

YOU WILL NEED

2 x 15ml spoons (2 tablespoons) of vegetable or olive oil

3 or 4 leeks, washed and sliced into circles

1 onion, peeled and chopped

450g (1lb) minced beef

2 x 15ml spoons (2 tablespoons) tomato puree

150ml (5fl oz) beef stock

4 or 5 potatoes, peeled

1 x 15ml spoon (1 tablespoon) butter

2 x 15ml spoons (2 tablespoons) milk

2oz (50g) cheddar cheese, grated

1. Put 1 tablespoon of the vegetable oil in a pan and cook the leeks for about five minutes till they're soft. Keep stirring them so they don't stick to the pan. Put the leeks into a dish or plate until later. You can use the same pan for the onions and mince.

2. Put the rest of the oil into the pan, and add the onions. Gently cook for about five minutes till they're soft, then add the mince. Break the mince up with a wooden spoon and keep stirring till the mince turns brown. Stir in the tomato puree and the beef stock. Cook on a low heat for about ten minutes. Keep giving it a stir. Put aside.

3. Put the potatoes in a pan of slightly salted water. Bring to the boil and simmer for twelve to eighteen minutes. After twelve minutes test them with a fork, if the fork slides in easily they are ready, if not boil for another two minutes and try again. Drain the potatoes. Use a potato masher to mash them up, then beat in the butter and milk with a wooden spoon.

4. It's time to put your dish together in an ovenproof dish. Start with the mince, and then layer your leeks on top, then the potatoes. Finish it off the grated cheese. Pop it into the oven for thirty minutes, enough time to wash the pots (boo), or watch the Simpsons (yay).

LEMONY CHICKEN WITH ROSEMARY

Serves 4
Preparation Time: 10 minutes
Cooking Time: 40 minutes

3 x 15ml spoons (3 tablespoons) wholemeal flour

½ x 5ml spoons (½ teaspoon) of cumin, same of turmeric

4 chicken supremes

3 x 15ml spoons (3 tablespoons) olive oil

grated rind and juice of 1 lemon

2 x 15ml spoons (2 tablespoons) clear honey

1 x 5ml spoon (1 teaspoon) fresh rosemary chopped

Heat the oven to 180C, 350F, GAS 4

1. Put the flour, turmeric and cumin into a plastic food bag and give it a good shake.

   Put the supremes into the bag one at a time and give each of them a bounce about till they are coated with the floury mix.

2. Pour the oil into a frying pan and fry the chicken supremes for a minute or so, turning over once so they are sealed on both sides. Lift the chicken out of the frying pan and put them into an ovenproof dish.

3. Time to make the sauce. Pour the honey into a bowl. Add the grated rind and juice of the lemon and the chopped rosemary. Slowly slide this into the pan. Watch it sizzle. Take the pan off the heat.

4. Pour the sauce over the chicken supremes, scraping the best sticky bits from the bottom as you do.

5. Cover the dish, use some tinfoil if it doesn't have a lid, and cook for forty minutes - enough time to do a spot of homework, while breathing in the smells of chicken and honey cooking.

Serve with new potatoes covered with parsley or a mixed salad. Or both.

SALMON FISHCAKES

YOU WILL NEED

400g (14oz) hot smoked salmon

1 egg, lightly beaten with a fork

4 or 5 potatoes, boiled and mashed

1 x 5ml spoon (1 teaspoon) parsley, chopped

1 x 15ml spoon (1 tablespoon) plain flour

2 x 15ml spoons (2 tablespoons) olive oil

Serves 4
Preparation Time: 15 minutes
Cooking Time: 10 minutes

1. Flake the salmon into little pieces in a bowl and add the egg and the potatoes. Mash them all together into a stiff mixture with a fork. Mix in the parsley.

2. Put the flour onto a plate. Scoop out a tablespoonful of the fish and potato mash and shape it into a patty - like a thick hamburger. Roll it into a ball, then flatten it a little. Dip the patty into the flour so it coats both sides.

3. Heat the oil in a frying pan and drop the fish cakes in. Turn them over when the underside gets crispy. Each side will take about four to five minutes to cook.

Serve with a green salad or a carrot salad.

LAMB KEBABS WITH BARBEQUE SAUCE

HoT

Serves 4

Preparation Time: 15 minutes

Cooking Time: 20 minutes

Marinating Time: 2 to 3 hours, or overnight if you have time

For the marinade

1 x 15ml spoon (1 tablespoon) honey

1 x 15ml spoon (1 tablespoon) lemon juice

1 x 5ml (1 teaspoon) soy sauce

4 x 5ml (4 teaspoons) Worcestershire sauce

1 clove of garlic, crushed

Ground black pepper

2 x 15ml spoons (2 tablespoons) olive oil

For the kebabs

225g (8oz) boneless lamb, diced

1 pepper, red or green, de-seeded and cut into squares

1 onion, peeled and sliced to same size as pepper

12 cherry tomatoes

12 button mushrooms

1. First make the marinade. Put all the ingredients into a small saucepan and stir over a gentle heat until everything is mixed together. Take off the heat and let cool. Put the lamb into a bowl and mix in the marinade, giving it a good stir. Put in the fridge and leave for at least two to three hours to let all the flavours mingle, overnight is even better.

2. Set the oven to 180C, 350F, GAS 5. Now thread the lamb, peppers and onions onto skewers. First on is a piece of meat, then a bit of pepper followed by a bit of onion. Keep going until the skewer is full.

3. Put the skewers in a roasting tin. If you have any marinade left drizzle it over the top and cook in the oven for twenty minutes. Keep turning them over every five minutes. After the first turn, time to make your tomato and mushroom skewers.

4. Thread the tomatoes and mushrooms onto skewers. Pop these into the oven to join the lamb for the last ten minutes.

Serve with a salad or on a bed of rice. Or, slip the meat and veg off the skewer and pack into pitta bread.

TOAD IN THE HOLE

Serves 4
Preparation Time: 5 minutes
Cooking Time: 30 to 35 minutes

For the batter

75g (3oz) plain flour

1 egg, lightly beaten with a fork

75g (3fl oz) semi-skimmed milk

salt and black pepper

1 x 15ml spoon (1 tablespoon) olive oil

8 sausages each cut into 3 pieces

Heat the oven to 220C, 425F, GAS 7

1. First make the batter. Sift the flour into a baking bowl. Beat the egg. Make a little well in the pile of flour and pour the beaten egg along with a little of the milk into it. Blend it with a fork till it goes into a smooth, thickish paste. Add more milk, beat, more milk, keep beating and more milk, still beating till all the milk is in your paste. Season with a little salt and a grating of pepper. Let the batter rest while the sausages start to cook.

2. Cover the bottom of a roasting tin with the oil and put in the sausages. Cook for ten minutes or until the sausages turn brown. Check them from time to time and turn them over so they don't stick to the bottom of the tin.

3. When they're done, take the roasting tin out of the oven, quickly pour the batter over the sausages and return to the oven. Cook for about twenty to twenty five minutes till the batter has risen and turned golden crispy brown.

4. Carefully cut into pieces and serve.

TAKE
CARE
NOT TO
BURN
YOUR
HANDS

SMOKED HADDOCK AND LEEK FLAN

4 smoked haddock fillets

100ml (4fl oz) semi skimmed milk

black pepper to taste

1 x savoury flan case, approx 20cm diameter

1 x 15ml spoon (1 tablespoon) olive oil

2 leeks, washed and sliced into circles

3 eggs, beaten

150ml (5fl oz) crème fraiche

2 x 15ml spoons (2 tablespoons) dill or parsley, chopped

Serves 4
Preparation Time: 10 minutes
Cooking Time: 40 minutes

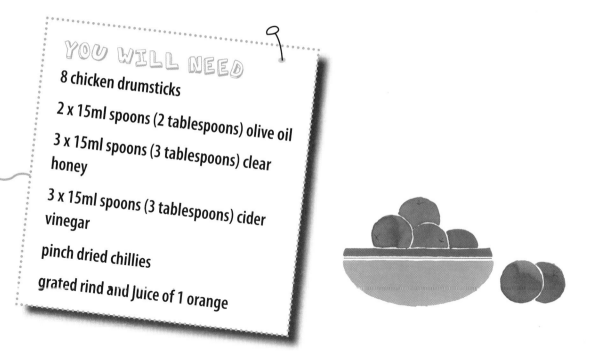

YOU WILL NEED

8 chicken drumsticks

2 x 15ml spoons (2 tablespoons) olive oil

3 x 15ml spoons (3 tablespoons) clear honey

3 x 15ml spoons (3 tablespoons) cider vinegar

pinch dried chillies

grated rind and juice of 1 orange

Heat the oven to 220C, 425F, GAS 7

1. Lay the drumsticks out in a row in the roasting tin. Pour the olive oil over the drumsticks, mixing them so they are all coated with oil.

2. Put the honey into a bowl with the cider vinegar, the dried chillies and the rind and juice of the orange. Mix together well. Spread this over the chicken and make sure each drumstick gets a good coating.

3. Put this in the oven. Go watch telly, or just hang about whistling. After ten minutes turn down the oven to 190C, 375F or GAS 5. Turn the drumsticks over so that the other side will turn crispy and golden.

4. Cook for another twenty minutes. They're sticky and great to eat with a salad, rice or baked potatoes. They're lovely cold too.

HONEY CHICKEN DRUMSTICKS

Serves 4
Preparation Time: 15 minutes
Cooking Time: 30 minutes

SPEEDY SUPPERS

Set the oven to 150C, 300F, GAS 2

1. Place the haddock into a pan with the milk and pepper and simmer for about eight minutes. Drain the pan, keeping back 2 tablespoons of the milk for later. Remove the oily skins from the haddock. Put the flan case onto a baking tray, then flake the fish into the flan case.

2. Put the olive oil into a pan and when it has heated a little pop the leeks in. Gently fry for about five minutes till soft. Scoop them into the flan case on top of the haddock.

3. Beat the eggs in a bowl; add the milk you kept back from the fish together with the crème fraiche and the dill or parsley. Pour this over the haddock and leeks.

4. Put in the oven for about thirty to thirty five minutes till it is golden brown and firm on top.

Serve with a simple salad.

SMOKED SALMON AND PRAWN QUICHE

Serves 4

Preparation Time: 5 minutes

Cooking Time: 40 minutes

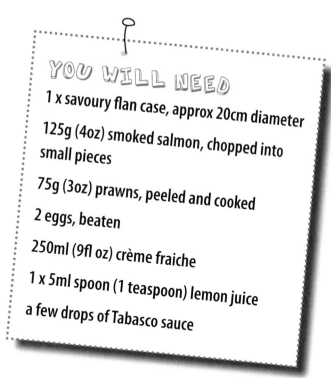

1 x savoury flan case, approx 20cm diameter

125g (4oz) smoked salmon, chopped into small pieces

75g (3oz) prawns, peeled and cooked

2 eggs, beaten

250ml (9fl oz) crème fraiche

1 x 5ml spoon (1 teaspoon) lemon juice

a few drops of Tabasco sauce

Set the oven to 180C, 350F, GAS 4

1. Put the flan on a baking tray. Scatter the smoked salmon and the prawns over the base.

2. Mix the eggs and crème fraiche in a bowl, then add the lemon juice and the Tabasco sauce. Pour this over the smoked salmon and the prawns.

3. Put the baking tray (and the flan, of course) into the oven for forty minutes till it is golden brown and firm on top.

ABERDEEN ANGUS BURGERS

Serves 4
Preparation Time: 5 minutes
Cooking Time: 12 minutes

YOU WILL NEED

250g (9oz) minced beef

1 x 15ml spoon (1 tablespoon) mustard (French is the mildest)

1 clove garlic (or 2 if you fancy), crushed

1 onion, chopped finely

pinch of salt and pepper

2 x 15ml spoons (2 tablespoons) olive oil

1. Flatten the mince out on a chopping board so it makes a large pancake. Spread the mustard over it, then the garlic. Sprinkle the chopped onion on top. Season with salt and pepper. Not too much, though.

2. Lift the edges of your meaty pancake and gradually fold it over keeping the ingredients together and slowly make it into a big ball. Divide this into four. Take each section, roll it up into a smaller ball, then, squeeze it into a burger shape.

3. Heat the olive oil in a frying pan. When the oil is hot drop each burger in. They'll need five to six minutes each side.

Nobody needs to be told how a burger is served. And nobody needs to be told how to eat it.

CHICKEN GOUJONS

Serves 4
Preparation Time: 5 minutes
Cooking Time: 6 minutes

YOU WILL NEED

4 x 15ml spoons (4 tablespoons) plain flour

25g (1oz) parmesan cheese, grated

1 x 5ml spoon (1 teaspoon) paprika

1 egg, beaten

4 x chicken breasts cut into strips of equal length and thickness

3 x 15ml spoons (3 tablespoons) vegetable oil or olive oil

1. Put the flour, parmesan and paprika into a bowl and mix well.

2. Put the beaten egg into another bowl.

3. Dip the chicken strips into the egg, getting them well coated. Transfer them, one by one into the floury mix.

4. Heat the oil in a frying pan and put the strips in. Give them about three minutes, then gently turn for another three minutes on the other side. They should be golden brown.

Serve them with a mayonnaise dip or in pitta bread with salad. The carrot salad goes well with this.

PENNE WITH BROCCOLI AND BACON

Serves 4

Preparation Time: 5 minutes

Cooking Time: 25 minutes

YOU WILL NEED

200g (7oz) penne pasta

200g (7oz) broccoli florets cut into small pieces

1 x 15ml spoon (1 tablespoon) olive oil

1 onion, peeled and chopped

2 cloves garlic, crushed

2 rashers of bacon, chopped

pinch of dried chillies

2 x 15ml spoons (2 tablespoons) parmesan cheese, grated

1. Put a pan of salted water onto boil. When it is bubbling at a gallop add the penne. Cook using the back of pack instructions. Half way through the cooking time, add the broccoli. Cook for remaining time then drain. Set aside.

2. In a frying pan, heat the oil then add the onions and cook gently for about five minutes till they are soft. Add the bacon and garlic and stir it all about to let the flavours mingle and the bacon cook. Lastly, put in the dried chillies.

3. Add your pasta and broccoli to the onion and bacon mix. The broccoli might break up, but that's OK. Mix everything well together and heat through.

Serve with a good scattering of parmesan cheese on top.

If you are vegetarian, this dish is still tasty without the bacon.

SMOKED HADDOCK POTS

Serves 4
Preparation Time: 15 minutes
Cooking Time: 20 minutes

SMOKE
HOOSE
ARBROATH

Smokies

4 haddock fillets

100ml (4fl oz) semi skimmed milk

8 cherry tomatoes

150ml (5fl oz) crème fraiche

2oz (50g) cheddar cheese, grated

Heat the oven to 180C, 350F, GAS 4

1. Put the haddock fillets into a pan and cover with the milk. Bring to the boil then gently simmer for about eight minutes until the fish is cooked. Leave to cool a little.

2. Carefully lift the fish out of the milk and put in a large bowl. Remove oily skins from the fish. Flake the fish with a fork so that it is in small pieces. Cut the tomatoes in half and add to the fish together with the crème fraiche. Mix everything together.

3. Divide the fish mixture between four ramekin dishes and sprinkle the cheese on top.

4. Place the dishes on a baking tray and put them into the oven for twenty minutes.

Serve with a simple green salad and brown bread to mop up the juices.

REMEMBER TO WASH YOUR HANDS

AFTER SCHOOL SNACKS

EGG IN A CUP

Serves 1
Cooking Time: 5 minutes

If you've had a bad day - someone's said something horrible to you in the playground, you've walked home through wind and rain carrying a heavy bag, you've a mountain of homework - then, egg in a cup is for you.

YOU WILL NEED
1 egg

a knob of butter

pinch of salt and pepper to taste

slice of bread for toast soldiers

butter for spreading

Put the egg into a pan and cover with water. Bring to the boil and simmer for five minutes.

Take pan off the heat and sit it under the cold tap. Run water on it to cool.

Lift the egg out. Tap it all over with a spoon, or tap it on the work surface to crack the shell.

Slip the egg out of its shell. Put it in a cup.

Cut the egg in half, add small knob of butter and mash it up with a fork.

Season with a little salt and a grinding of pepper.

Make toast. Butter it. Cut it into long fingers.

Now eat.

This is old-fashioned comfort food.

CHEESE ON TOAST

Serves 1

Cooking Time: 3 to 4 minutes

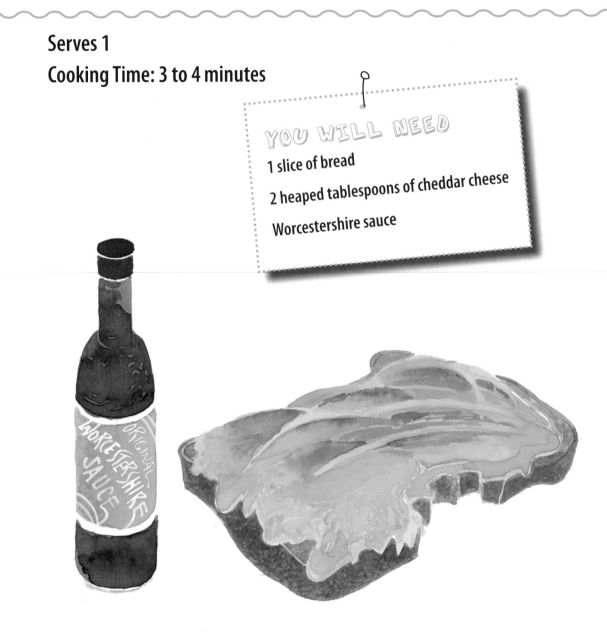

Toast one side of the bread under the grill.

Grate the cheese and heap it onto the untoasted side of the bread. Splash a dash of the sauce on top.

Shove it back under the grill and when the cheese is bubbling and turning brown, it's ready.

If you fancy trying a variation then chop up an onion very finely. Mix together with some chopped herbs - thyme, basil or parsley are good. Then put this mixture on top of the cheese before you put it under the grill.

MACKEREL PATE

Serves 4
Preparation Time: 5 minutes

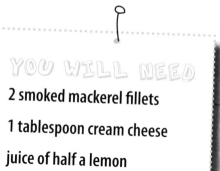

Remove the oily skin from the fillets. It tears off easily. Now, crumble the fish into small pieces, heap into a bowl and crush them with a fork.

Scoop in the cheese and mix it through. Stir in the lemon juice.

This is excellent on hot buttered toast or on oatcakes.

MR WATSON'S BEANS ON TOAST

Serves 4
Preparation Time: 5 minutes
Cooking Time: 10 minutes

YOU WILL NEED

1 tablespoon olive oil

1 small onion, peeled and chopped

1 red pepper, deseeded, sliced and chopped

pinch dried chillies

1 can of baked beans

4 slices bread

butter for spreading

Put the oil in a small pan, heat then add the onion and pepper. Cook for about ten minutes, stirring. Add the baked beans and dried chillies and keep stirring so the onions and pepper are well mixed through the beans.

Put four slices of bread into the toaster. When they have popped out, spread with butter and heap a pile of the mix on top of each one.

STICKY SAUSAGES

YOU WILL NEED

8 sausages

2 tablespoons maple syrup

1 tablespoon dijon mustard

Serves 4

Preparation Time: 5 minutes

Cooking Time: 30 minutes

Set the oven to 200C, 400F, GAS 6

Cut the sausages into chunks and put them on a lightly greased baking tray.

Mix the maple syrup and the mustard in a bowl, then pour over the sausage chunks making sure they are all well coated.

Put in the oven for thirty minutes - about four or five or maybe even six CD tracks. Or attempt some homework, though it's hard when you are distracted by the sweet, sticky sausagey aroma.

HERO SANDWICH

Serves One Very Hungry Person

Preparation Time: 10 minutes

This is fun to make. You can toast the bread, or not. It's up to you.

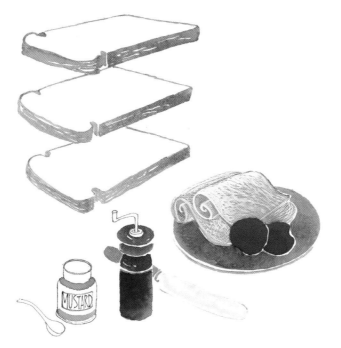

YOU WILL NEED

1 egg, boiled

a good clipping of cress from little box it comes in

2 tablespoons mayonnaise

3 slices of bread, wholemeal is best

small knob of butter

2 slices ham

a little mustard

1 tomato

S is for Sandwich

Chop up the egg and in bowl, mix it with the cress and mayonnaise.

Toast your bread, if that's how you want it and spread with margarine or butter.

Now assemble your sarnie.

Bread (or toast), egg mixture, bread, ham, mustard and tomato, bread. Actually, you don't have to stop here. You can make more layers, your sandwich can reach the ceiling. Best not, though. The sandwich might topple, you could run out of bread and not have any left for toast in the morning. There could be bickering about that.

You can, of course, make any filling you like - bacon, lettuce and tomato is good. Ham and grated cheese and tomato, soft cheese and slices of apple, tuna and mayo. There are loads when you start thinking about them.

CLASSIC SUBMARINE SANDWICH

Serves One Very Hungry Person
Preparation Time: 5 minutes

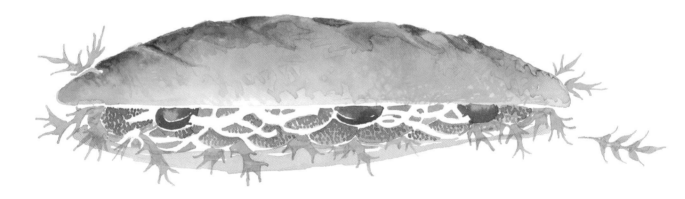

Slice the baguette longways. Start with the margarine or butter on the bottom half, layer on the salami, then the mozzarella cheese in slices. After that comes the onion cut in thin rings, followed by slices of tomato and the salad leaves. Finally, spoon on the mayonnaise.

Also, remember these recipes aren't written in stone. You can change things if you don't like them. You can use ham or chicken if you don't like salami, and, whatever kind of cheese is your favourite. Try to keep the salad, though, you know it's good for you.

WASH ROOT VEGETABLES BEFORE YOU SCRAPE OR PEEL THEM

VEGETABLES

CARROT SALAD

Serves 4

Preparation Time: 5 minutes

1. Place the grated carrots in a bowl.

2. Put the honey into another bowl, add the vinegar, stirring as you go, then the oil, keep stirring. Your mixture should go quite thick.

3. Pour your dressing over the carrots. Mix it all about till all the carrots are coated and a little glossy. Season with black pepper.

You can add other things if you like - raisins, parsley, coriander or nuts.

YOU WILL NEED

3 large carrots, peeled and grated

1 x 15ml spoon (1 tablespoon) clear honey

3 x 15ml spoons (3 tablespoons) cider vinegar

1 x 15ml spoon (1 tablespoon) olive oil

black pepper to taste

This is a juicy salad that goes with just about anything.

It's quick and easy to make.

APPLE AND CHICKEN CRUNCH

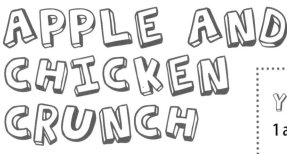

Serves 2
Preparation Time: 5 minutes

YOU WILL NEED

1 apple, chopped

1 stick celery chopped

125g (4oz) cooked chicken

1 x 15ml spoon (1 tablespoon) mayonnaise

Put everything into a bowl and stir together. That's it. The amounts don't have to be exact. If you don't have the exact amount of roast chicken, it works with less and also works with more. It's a laid back recipe.

Good in a sandwich or in a baked potato.

This is a good way to use up any left over roast chicken

SQUISHY PEAS

Serves 4

Preparation Time: 1 minute

Cooking Time: 4 to 5 minutes

YOU WILL NEED

450g (1lb) frozen peas

25g (1oz) butter

1 x 15ml spoon (1tablespoon) crème fraiche

pinch of black pepper

Easy peezy pea recipe

1. Put a pan of salted water on to boil. When it is seething and bubbling, drop in the peas. Please remember to take them out of the pack first.

2. When the peas rise to the top of the pan, about four to five minutes, take them off the heat and drain them. Put them back into the hot pan.

3. Drop in the butter, crème fraiche and pepper. Then mix them all together with a hand blender. That's it. Now eat.

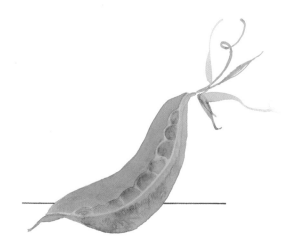

COLESLAW CRUNCH

Serves 4
Preparation Time: 5 minutes
Chilling Time: 30 minutes

1. Place brussels sprouts or cabbage, carrots, apple, celery, raisins and grapes into a bowl.

2. Add the lemon juice and the mayonnaise and stir until all ingredients are smothered with mayonnaise.

3. Chill for about thirty minutes, then serve.

Good with burgers.

YOU WILL NEED

6 brussels sprouts, shredded or quarter a small cabbage, shredded

4 carrots, peeled and grated

1 apple, grated

1 stick celery, finely chopped

2 x 15ml spoons (2 tablespoons) raisins

8 seedless white grapes

juice of ½ lemon

2 x 15ml spoons (2 tablespoons) mayonnaise

REALLY, REALLY, EASY CAULIFLOWER CHEESE

Serves 4
Preparation Time: 5 minutes
Cooking Time: 15 minutes

YOU WILL NEED

1 cauliflower, chopped into small florets

150g (5oz) crème fraiche

75g (3oz) parmesan cheese

50g (2oz) cheddar cheese

1. Bring a pan of slightly salted water to the boil. When it is bubbling slide in the cauliflower. Don't drop it in - you don't want to get splashed with hot water. Boil for four to five minutes or till a fork slides in easily.

2. Take it off the heat and drain. Set aside.

3. Now make the cheese sauce. Scoop the crème fraiche into a bowl and add half of the parmesan cheese and mix together. That's it. It will look a little lumpy, but as soon as you add this to the cauliflower, it will melt.

4. Put the cooked cauliflower into an oven proof dish, spoon the creamy sauce over the top. Sprinkle the rest of the parmesan cheese and the cheddar cheese over the top.

5. Put under a hot grill until the cheesy top is golden brown. This will only take a few minutes. Eat. It's too easy for words.

Serves 4
Preparation Time: 5 minutes
Cooking Time: 20 minutes

A traditional Scottish vegetable accompaniment and a great way to use up left over vegetables

25g (2oz) unsalted butter

1 onion, finely chopped

6 or 7 potatoes, boiled and mashed

small cabbage, shredded and cooked

1 x 15ml (1 tablespoon) chopped chives

50g (5oz) grated cheese

1. Melt the butter in a large pan and fry the onion. Cook gently for five minutes till soft.

2. Add the potatoes, cabbage and chives, mix well. Cook gently for five to ten minutes.

3. Season well and put into an oven proof dish. Cover with the cheese and put under a hot grill till the cheese is golden.

BAKED POTATOES

Preparation Time: 5 minutes

Cooking Time: 45 to 60 minutes

YOU WILL NEED

1 baked potato per person

Heat the oven to 190C, 375F, GAS 5

1. If you are doing more than one baked potato, try to pick some that are roughly the same size so they'll all be cooked through at the same time. Wash them, dry with a paper towel and prick them here and there with a fork. This helps them to cook more quickly, and it stops them exploding in the oven.

2. Put them straight into the oven, they cook better if they are not on a baking tray.

3. They'll be done in forty five to sixty minutes. Time to do some homework or play half a football match. The potatoes are ready when a fork slides into them easily. Don't worry about them. Baking potatoes are easy going, they don't mind spending a bit too long in the oven.

4. When you are ready to eat them, split them open, add a little butter, salt and pepper and either eat like that or heap on some grated cheese, baked beans or anything else you fancy!

They are also good with the Carrot Salad, Coleslaw Crunch, Apple and Chicken Crunch, Cauliflower and Cheese...

GET A GROWN-UP TO HELP

DESSERTS

PEAR AND RASPBERRY TORTE

Serves 6
Preparation Time: 5 minutes
Cooking Time: 30 minutes

YOU WILL NEED
225g (8oz) short crust pastry

125g (4oz) marzipan (chilled in the fridge)

2 large pears

1 egg

2 x 15ml spoons (2 tablespoons) caster sugar

225g (8oz) raspberries

Heat the oven to 190C, 375F, GAS 5

1. Roll out the pastry till it is quite thin. Put a large dinner plate on top of it and, with a small vegetable knife, cut round it. Lift away the outer pastry, take off the plate and you should have a circle of pastry. Put this onto a greased baking tray.

2. Grate the marzipan. This is easy to do if the marzipan is cold. Now, scatter the gratings on top of the pastry, but don't spread it right to the edge. Leave a gap of about 3 - 5cm all the way round. Peel and slice the pears and put them on top of the marzipan.

3. Beat the egg in a small bowl or mug and brush the edge of your pastry ring with it. Now flute the edges. That is, make a pattern by pressing the edge all the way round with your thumb. Sprinkle the sugar over the whole torte and put it into the oven. Bake for twenty minutes.

4. Take the baking tray out of the oven and sprinkle your raspberries over the top of the torte. Put it back into the oven for a further ten minutes. After that it will be ready to eat. Or you can leave it and have it cold.

It's good with ice cream, cream or custard.

FROZEN GRAPE PUDDING

large bunch seedless grapes

50g (2oz) sugar (raw cane is good but any sugar will do)

150ml (5fl oz) whipping cream

2 x 5ml spoons (2 teaspoons) vanilla essence (optional)

50g (2oz) demerara sugar

Serves 4

Preparation Time: 10 minutes

Freezing Time: 3 hours

This is really easy

1. First pull the grapes from their stalks. Now, wash them by putting them into a colander and rinsing them under the cold tap. Shake them about to dry them off and put them in a bowl and put half of the sugar over them. Mix this through so the grapes are slightly coated.

2. Using an electric or hand beater, beat the cream with the rest of the sugar till it is thick. When you lift out the beater, the cream should make soft peaks. Add the vanilla essence and mix it through.

3. Put the cream into the bowl with the grapes and mix it through so you have a creamy grapey mixture. Put this into the freezer and leave till it is frozen. This will take about three hours, so if you fancy having this for supper, remember to make it early.

4. When your grape pudding is frozen, take it out of the freezer and scatter the demerara sugar over the top. Now put it under a hot grill. In a few minutes, not long at all - so, don't go off and watch a quick bit of telly, keep an eye on it - the sugar will have melted and turned into a thick, crunchy caramel. The cream will, of course, have melted a little round the edges, but in the middle it will still be grapey and frozen.

RASPBERRY SMASH

Serves 4
Preparation Time: 5 minutes

1. Crush each meringue into the bottom of each of four glasses

2. Put an equal amount of raspberries on top of each crushed meringue. Unless nobody is looking then you can give yourself more.

3. Put a scoop of ice cream on top of the raspberries.

4. Pour over the cream.

   Enjoy.

Easiest
pudding
ever

THREE CHOCOLATE FRUIT FONDUE

Serves 6
Preparation Time: 5 minutes
Cooking Time: 5 to 10 minutes

YOU WILL NEED
1 bar milk chocolate
1 bar plain chocolate
1 bar white chocolate
Selection of fruit - raspberries, strawberries, apples, bananas and any other fruit you like washed and chopped up.

1. Break each of the chocolate bars into a separate ramekin dish.

2. Put water to the depth of about 5cm into a large shallow pan and put the dishes into it. Put the ramekins into the water and bring to a gentle simmer - just slightly bubbling.

3. Keep a careful watch on the chocolate as it melts.

4. When the chocolate has melted, take the dishes out of the water and put onto a tea towel to dry their bottoms. Now, put them on a big plate surrounded by the chopped fruit.

   Using a fork, dip a bit of fruit into the different chocolates and see which combination you like best.

PANCAKES

125g (4oz) self-raising flour

small pinch salt

25g (1oz) caster sugar

1 egg

150ml (5fl oz) milk

Serves 4
Preparation Time: 5 minutes
Cooking Time: 10 minutes

You'll also need
a large griddle or
frying pan

1. Sift the four and salt and sugar into a bowl.

2. Crack the egg into another bowl, add the milk and beat together with a fork.

3. Make a well in the flour and slowly, slowly pour in the milk and egg mixing all the while with a fork till you have a smooth batter. If any lumps form, crush them against the side of the bowl then mix them in.

4. Heat the griddle or frying pan till it is hot enough to quickly sizzle a little bit of butter.

5. Test to see if the pan is hot enough by putting a fairy sized pancake into it. It should cook very quickly, almost as soon as it hits the pan.

6. Drop the batter, a tablespoonful at a time, into the pan. Cook for about one minute, or till the surface starts to bubble. Then turn over and cook for another minute.

7. Once you get the hang of this you can make a huge batch of pancakes while everyone lines up to get one. Make sure you aren't so busy dropping dollops of batter into the pan, and flipping them over that you don't get one or two for yourself.

PLUM CRUMBLE

Serves 6
Preparation Time: 15 minutes
Cooking Time: 40 minutes

YOU WILL NEED

450g (1lb) plums

1 x 15ml spoon (1 tablespoon) honey

For the crumble

150g (5oz) plain flour

125g (4oz) butter

50g (2oz) dark brown sugar

50g (2oz) rolled oats

150ml (5fl oz) double cream or crème fraiche to serve

Heat the oven to 190C, 375F, GAS 5

1. Cut the plums in half and take out the stones. Then cut each half into about four pieces.

2. Put the plums and honey into a deep pan over a low heat. Stir gently till the honey melts and the plums are gooey and soft. If the plums are very ripe this might take five minutes, if the plums are quite hard it might take about ten minutes.

Set aside.

3. For the crumble mixture rub the butter into the flour. This is easiest done in a big bowl with the butter cut into small pieces. Rub the butter into the flour with your finger tips until it looks like breadcrumbs. Then stir in the sugar and the oats.

4. Pile the plum mixture into an oven proof dish and cover with the crumble topping.

5. Put into the oven for about forty minutes till the crumble is crisp and golden and the plums are bubbling through.

Serve hot with lots of double cream.

VERY EASY CHEESECAKE

Serves 6
Preparation Time: 40 minutes
Chilling Time: overnight

YOU WILL NEED

8 digestive biscuits, crushed

50g (2oz) butter, melted

125g (4oz) soft cream cheese

125g (4oz) mascarpone cheese

75g (3oz) caster sugar

grated rind and juice of 1 lemon

small punnet strawberries

100ml (4fl oz) double cream

This delicious dessert needs to set in the fridge for a few hours, preferably overnight.

You can use lots of different fruits on the top. Raspberries or sliced banana are particularly yummy.

1. Crush the biscuits. You can either crumble them with your fingers or put them in a plastic food bag and crush with a wooden spoon. Put the crushed biscuits into a bowl and mix in the melted butter.

2. Put the mixture in a flan dish or a round loose bottom cake tin (about 20 cm diameter). Use your fingers or the back of a spoon to spread the mixture evenly and press it down into the dish. Put into the fridge to set for about thirty minutes.

3. Mix together the soft cream cheese, mascarpone cheese, sugar and the rind and juice of the lemon. Use a fork and whip around until the mixture is smooth. Pour over the biscuit mixture. Leave until it is set, best if you can leave overnight.

4. When you are ready to serve slice the strawberries and pile on top of the cheesecake. Then cut the cheesecake into slices and serve.

Even more delicious with double cream poured over the top!

January 25th is a time for celebrating the work of one of the most famous poets, Robbie Burns.

Celebrate Burns Day with this three course menu, and don't forget to recite a few poems by Robbie Burns!

MENU
Cullen Skink
Haggis, Neeps and Tatties
Granny Green's Clootie Dumpling

BURNS SUPPER

CULLEN SKINK

Serves 4

Preparation Time: 5 minutes

Cooking Time: 25 minutes

YOU WILL NEED

25g (1oz) butter

1 onion, peeled and chopped

4 or 5 small potatoes, peeled and diced

300ml (½ pint) milk

300ml (½ pint) water

225g (8oz) smoked haddock

salt and pepper to taste

1 x 15ml spoon (1 tablespoon) parsley, chopped

1. Melt the butter in a large pan. Add the onion and cook for about five minutes till it is soft. Add the potatoes and cook for another three to four minutes.

2. Add the milk and water, stir well and bring to the boil. Simmer gently for ten minutes.

3. Take the skin off the haddock and cut into bite size pieces. Carefully add to the pan and simmer gently for five minutes, till the fish is cooked. Season with a little salt and black pepper.

4. When you've served the soup into bowls, sprinkle a good scattering of parsley on the top of each one and serve with crusty bread.

HAGGIS, NEEPS AND TATTIES

Serves 4
Preparation Time: 10 minutes
Cooking Time: 60 minutes

YOU WILL NEED

1 haggis

1 neep (swede/turnip)

7 or 8 tatties (potatoes)

2 x 15ml (2 tablespoons) milk

2 x 5ml spoons (2 teaspoons) salt

black pepper

50g (2 oz) butter

Haggis

1. First buy a haggis. Cook it according to the instructions on the pack.

2. Peel the neep. This can be hard. But you can get half a neep which is easier to handle. Once it is peeled, cut it into cubes and boil in water with one teaspoon of salt for about ten to fifteen minutes.

3. Peel the tatties and cut so they are all roughly the same size. Put into a pan of salted water and bring to the boil and simmer for twelve to eighteen minutes. After twelve minutes test them with a fork, if the fork slides in easily they are ready, if not boil for another two minutes and try again.

4. When the neep is soft, drain off the water, put the neep back into the pot and mash it with a potato masher. Then add half the butter and a grinding of black pepper and mix through. Do the same with the tatties, but also beat in two tablespoons of milk with a wooden spoon.

5. Take the haggis out of the pot or the oven. Pierce the haggis skin and cut the haggis open. Serve the haggis with the neeps and tatties.

GRANNY GREEN'S CLOOTIE DUMPLING

Serves 8
Preparation Time: 10 minutes
Cooking Time: 3 to 4 hours

YOU WILL NEED

450g (1lb) plain flour

225g (8oz) sugar

2 x 15ml spoons (2 tablespoons) ground mixed spice

175g (6oz) raisins

175g (6oz) sultanas

125g (4oz) currants

1 x 5ml spoon (1 teaspoon) bicarbonate soda

50g (2oz) butter, melted

2 x 15ml spoons (2 tablespoons) syrup or treacle

75ml (3fl oz) milk

A little extra flour for sprinkling on the clootie dumpling cloth

MUCKLE CLOOTIE CLOTH

1. Put all the flour, sugar, mixed spice and the dried fruit into a big baking bowl and mix together. Mix in the bicarbonate of soda.

2. Stir in the butter and the syrup or treacle. This will need some serious stirring.

3. Add the milk, more serious stirring. When the mixture drops softly from the spoon, you have the right consistency.

4. Soak a muslin cloth or clean pillow case (your clootie cloth) and wring it out till it is slightly damp. Spread it out and sprinkle with the extra flour.

5. Put the cloth into a big bowl, opened up and ready to receive the clootie mixture. Spoon the mix into the cloth, gather the edges of the top together and tie firmly with a bit string. Leave enough room for the dumpling to expand, as expand it will. Clootie dumplings are prone to expanding.

6. Take the tied up cloth out of the bowl and put into a big pan that has a good layer of boiling water at the bottom. Boil for three to four hours, checking regularly that the water hasn't dried up. If it has, top up with boiling water from the kettle.

7. Once the dumpling is ready, take it from the pan, peel away the cloth and hello, clootie dumpling.

8. Cut into slices and serve with a sprinkling of sugar or custard. If there is any leftovers, either serve as a snack or gently fry the slices in a little butter.

The Cullen Skink is not a funny wee beastie who lives under a stone just outside Cullen - jumping up and shouting BOO! No, no, this is only a rumour - it's a delicious soup!

St Andrews Day is celebrated on the 30th November. St Andrew is the patron saint of Scotland. Celebrate this day with a Scottish menu and after eating have a wee ceilidh, sing a few songs and dance a few jigs!

MENU

Smoked Salmon and Mackerel Parcels
Venison Cassoulet
Trifle

SMOKED SALMON AND MACKEREL PARCELS

Serves 4

Preparation Time: 10 minutes

Chilling Time: 2 hours

225g (8oz) smoked salmon slices

2 smoked mackerel fillets

25g (1oz) butter

75g (3oz) soft cream cheese

1 x 15ml spoon (1 tablespoon) lemon juice

1. Trim the smoked salmon slices into even rectangles. Keep the trimmings for later.

2. Remove the oily skins from the mackerel. Put in a bowl with the butter, cream cheese, lemon juice and salmon trimmings. Blend with a fork or hand blend till smooth.

3. Place this mixture a spoonful at a time onto the smoked salmon slices and fold up each end so you have a parcel. You can use cocktail sticks to keep them together if you want. Don't eat these, please.

4. Put the parcels into the fridge for about two hours to set.

These are good with a salad or oatcakes. Or both.

VENISON SAUSAGE CASSOULET

Serves 4

Preparation Time: 5 minutes

Cooking Time: 1 hour and 15 minutes

Heat the oven to 190C, 375F, GAS 5

1. Cut each sausage into about three chunks.

   Heat the olive oil in a large frying pan, add onion and cook for about five minutes until it is soft, stirring now and then.

2. Add the garlic and the sausage chunks and fry, gently moving things about the pan so they don't stick to the bottom. After about ten minutes the sausages should be brown all over.

3. Add the chopped tomatoes and the cannelloni beans. Stir in. Add half of the parsley. Season everything with a little salt and a good grinding of black pepper.

4. Transfer all this into a casserole dish that has a lid. Put that lid on and pop into the oven for fifty to sixty minutes.

5. Serve the venison cassoulet with chopped fresh parsley scattered over the top.

   Good with crunchy bread and a green salad.

TRIFLE

Serves 4
Preparation Time: 10 minutes
Chilling Time: 2 hours

The jelly takes two hours to set in the fridge so you need to have plenty of time before you want to eat this!

1 Swiss roll

1 x 420g fruit cocktail

1 packet strawberry jelly, dissolved using the back of pack instructions

1 x 425g can ready made custard

600 ml (1pint) double cream

1 x 15ml spoon (1 tablespoon) caster sugar

1. Cut the Swiss roll into slices and cover the bottom of a bowl with them.

   Spread the fruit cocktail over these Swiss roll slices. Now pour over the made up, but not yet set, jelly.

2. Put the bowl into the fridge and wait for the jelly to set. This will take about two hours. Enough time to watch some Dr Who or play a game of football or hang about chatting to some friends.

3. When the jelly has set, pour the custard on top. Just before serving the trifle, whip the cream with a tablespoon of sugar in a large bowl using a hand whisk or an electric mixer. Spoon the cream over the top of the jelly.

   If you want you can sprinkle this with hundreds and thousands.

From top left - Lettuce, Tomato, Ox Horn and Bell Peppers, Pumpkin,
Marrow, Gherkins, Fennel, Runner Beans, Peas, Potato,
Broccoli, Cabbage, Corn On The Cob, Leek, Chilli, Parsnip, Sprouts,
Kohl rabi, Celery, Carrot, Radish, Neep,
Cucumber, Cauliflower, Butternut Squash, Garlic, Courgette, Rhubarb,
Onions, Beetroot